Regional Folklore

North American Folklore

Children's Folklore
Christmas and Santa Claus Folklore
Contemporary Folklore
Ethnic Folklore
Family Folklore
Firefighters' Folklore
Folk Arts and Crafts
Folk Customs
Folk Dance
Folk Fashion
Folk Festivals
Folk Games
Folk Medicine
Folk Music
Folk Proverbs and Riddles
Folk Religion
Folk Songs
Folk Speech
Folk Tales and Legends
Food Folklore
Regional Folklore

North American Folklore

Regional Folklore

BY ANN E. VITALE

Mason Crest Publishers

Mason Crest Publishers Inc.
370 Reed Road
Broomall, Pennsylvania 19008
(866) MCP-BOOK (toll free)
www.masoncrest.com

First printing
1 2 3 4 5 6 7 8 9 10
Library of Congress Cataloging-in-Publication Data on file at the Library of Congress.
ISBN 1-59084-349-5
1-59084-328-2 (series)

Design by Lori Holland.
Composition by Bytheway Publishing Services, Binghamton, New York.
Cover design by Joe Gilmore.
Printed and bound in the Hashemite Kingdom of Jordan.

Picture credits:
Corbis: pp. 12, 51, 68, 71, 74, 78, 81
J. Rowe: pp. 10, 11, 18, 20, 23, 24, 25, 40, 41, 44, 48, 60, 62, 86, 88, 96, 99
Map Resources: pp. 6, 16, 26, 36, 36, 46, 58, 66, 76, 84, 94
Photo Disc: pp. 8, 28, 38, 92
Cover: "Three Old Salts" by J. F. Kernan © 1932 SEPS: Licensed by Curtis Publishing, Indianapolis, IN. www.curtispublishing.com

Contents

Folklore grows from long-ago seeds. Just as an acorn sends down roots even as it shoots up leaves across the sky, folklore is rooted deeply in the past and yet still lives and grows today. It spreads through our modern world with branches as wide and sturdy as any oak's; it grounds us in yesterday even as it helps us make sense of both the present and the future.

Introduction

by Dr. Alan Jabbour

WHAT DO A TALE, a joke, a fiddle tune, a quilt, a jig, a game of jacks, a saint's day procession, a snake fence, and a Halloween costume have in common? Not much, at first glance, but all these forms of human creativity are part of a zone of our cultural life and experience that we sometimes call "folklore."

The word "folklore" means the cultural traditions that are learned and passed along by ordinary people as part of the fabric of their lives and culture. Folklore may be passed along in verbal form, like the urban legend that we hear about from friends who assure us that it really happened to a friend of their cousin. Or it may be tunes or dance steps we pick up on the block, or ways of shaping things to use or admire out of materials readily available to us, like that quilt our aunt made. Often we acquire folklore without even fully realizing where or how we learned it.

Though we might imagine that the word "folklore" refers to cultural traditions from far away or long ago, we actually use and enjoy folklore as part of our own daily lives. It is often ordinary, yet we often remember and prize it because it seems somehow very special. Folklore is culture we share with others in our communities, and we build our identities through the sharing. Our first shared identity is family identity, and family folklore such as shared meals or prayers or songs helps us develop a sense of belonging. But as we grow older we learn to belong to other groups as well. Our identities may be ethnic, religious, occupational, or regional—or all of these, since no one has only one cultural identity. But in every case, the identity is anchored and strengthened by a variety of cultural traditions in which we participate and share with our neighbors. We feel the threads of connection with people we know, but the threads extend far beyond our own immediate communities. In a real sense, they connect us in one way or another to the world.

Folklore possesses features by which we distinguish ourselves from each other. A certain dance step may be African American, or a certain story urban, or a certain hymn Protestant, or a certain food preparation Cajun. Folklore can distinguish us, but at the same time it is one of the best ways we introduce ourselves to each other. We learn about new ethnic groups on the North American landscape by sampling their cuisine, and we enthusiastically adopt musical ideas from other communities. Stories, songs, and visual designs move from group to group, enriching all people in the process. Folklore thus is both a sign of identity, experienced as a special marker of our special groups, and at the same time a cultural coin that is well spent by sharing with others beyond our group boundaries.

Folklore is usually learned informally. Somebody, somewhere, taught us that jump rope rhyme we know, but we may have trouble remembering just where we got it, and it probably wasn't in a book that was assigned as homework. Our world has a domain of formal knowledge, but folklore is a domain of knowledge and culture that is learned by sharing and imitation rather than formal instruction. We can study it formally—that's what we are doing now!—but its natural arena is in the informal, person-to-person fabric of our lives.

Not all culture is folklore. Classical music, art sculpture, or great novels are forms of high art that may contain folklore but are not themselves folklore. Popular music or art may be built on folklore themes and traditions, but it addresses a much wider and more diverse audience than folk music or folk art. But even in the world of popular and mass culture, folklore keeps popping up around the margins. E-mail is not folklore—but an e-mail smile is. And college football is not folklore—but the wave we do at the stadium is.

This series of volumes explores the many faces of folklore throughout the North American continent. By illuminating the many aspects of folklore in our lives, we hope to help readers of the series to appreciate more fully the richness of the cultural fabric they either possess already or can easily encounter as they interact with their North American neighbors.

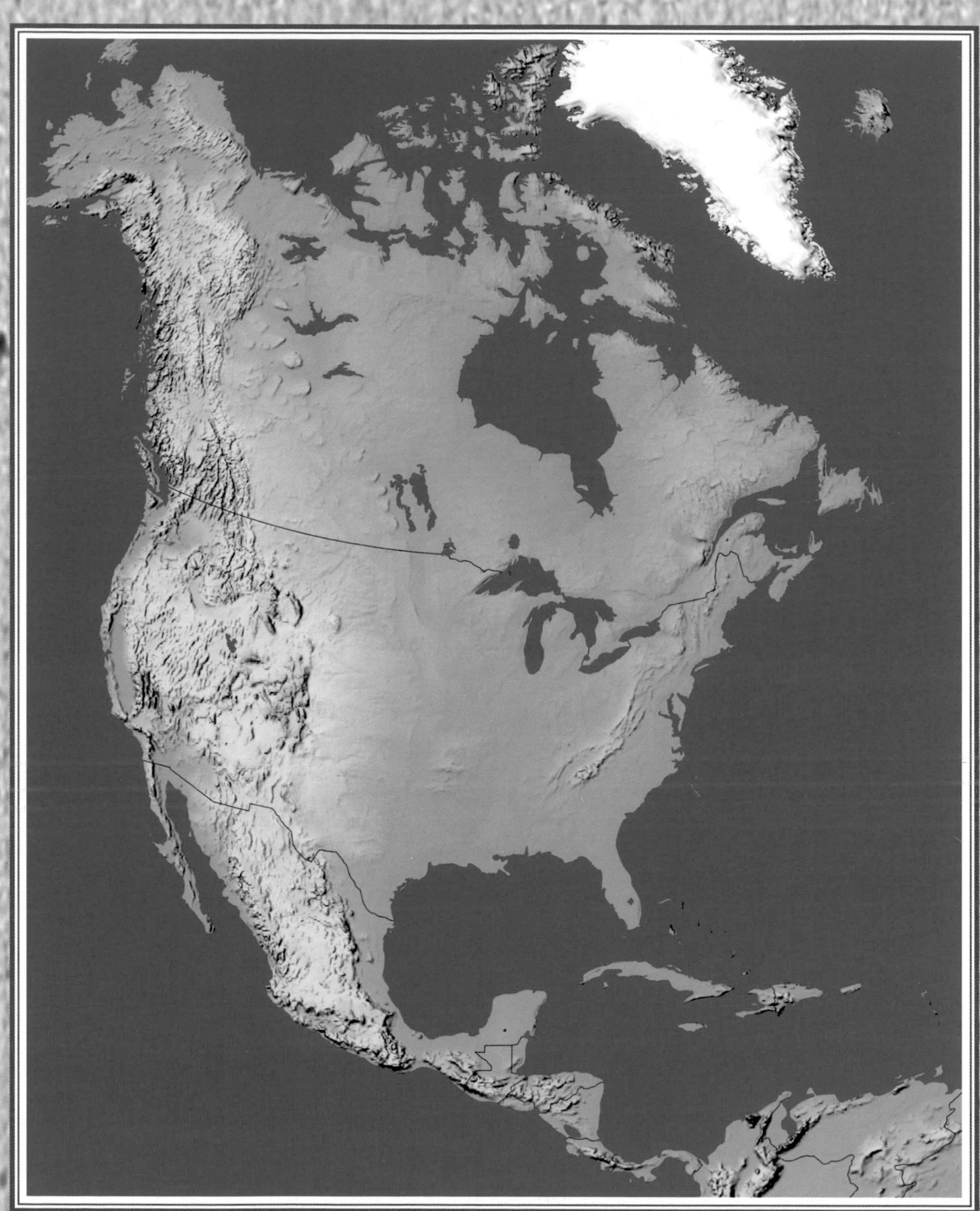

Folklore flourishes from region to region across North America.

ONE

Suitcases Full of Stories

The Folklore of North Americans

The weather and the land itself shaped the folklore that grew in the regions of North America.

WHAT IS folklore? Folklore is sometimes defined as a body of knowledge that relates to daily life. And who are folk? They are ordinary people. Not the royal family, not the wealthy elite, not the intellectual aristocracy of a nation. In fact, many folktales poke fun at the prestigious and the powerful. American settlers left Europe and then fought the Revolutionary War to escape from tyranny and control by strong kings and rich land holders. In the popular trickster stories, the clever human or animal trickster always won by outthinking the stronger enemy. The Yankee Peddler was one such North American trickster.

THE stagecoach, with the Yankee Peddler and five other passengers on board, rolled over the dusty roads of Oklahoma toward Texas. In a few miles they would stop for a bite to eat at a roadside tavern in a tiny town. The horses could be watered while the mail was put on board the stage.

Everyone was hungry and looking forward to the break, when one passenger said, "Don't get too excited. I've been here before and you'll be lucky if you get a few bites of food and a swallow of water before the stage is ready to leave. It's a scheme between the driver and the tavern owner."

"Scheme or not, I intend to have a rest and a good dinner," replied the Yankee Peddler.

"If you try that, the stage will leave without you," said the first man.

Now this Yankee had been around and was a known trickster himself, but these folks obviously hadn't heard of him.

"I'll bet you the price of everyone's dinner that I'll have a full meal and still continue my travels with you," the Peddler boasted.

"You'll lose for sure," the other man replied, "but I'll take your money, even though you're a Yankee and don't know much about our ways." Just as the stage pulled up at the tavern, the two men gave the bet money to a lady to hold.

The tavern owner collected 50 cents from each person at the door and promised a turkey dinner that wasn't quite ready yet. Then, sure enough, just as the meal was served and the passengers had hardly eaten two bites, the stage driver ran in yelling that the mail was behind schedule and he couldn't wait another minute to leave. The travelers hurried out, all except the Yankee. He calmly ate the first and then the second course.

"Better hurry. The stage won't wait," the tavern keeper warned.

"I don't care. I'm going to eat my fill." The Yankee cocked his head and listened to the rattle of the stagecoach wheels as they pulled away from the tavern. Then he calmly took another helping of turkey and asked for a spoon for more gravy.

"Why, there were half a dozen silver spoons here a minute ago." The tavern keeper stared at the table. The only folks who could have taken the spoons were on the stage, so the stingy tav-

The Yankee Peddler was a wily and clever trickster.

The Yankee Peddler is an example of a trickster—and there are other trickster stories told all across North America. In the South there are Br'er Rabbit stories galore. Clever Jack tales are also Southern in origin. Pecos Bill is a familiar folk trickster in Texas and other parts of the Southwest. He wins battles with wildcats, cattle rustlers, and windstorms by using his intelligence. Coyote stories, yet another set of trickster tales, are most influenced by American Indian culture. You'll also find Kokopelli there as well. He is the hunchbacked, flute playing prehistoric figure who carries tricks in his sack.

ern keeper rushed out to his horse and chased after the stage. In about 20 minutes the whole party was back, clattering and hollering, just as the Peddler finished his coffee and a second piece of pear cactus pie.

The owner made everyone get off the stagecoach and come inside to be searched and maybe arrested. While they waited, the Peddler suggested they all sit down and enjoy the dinner for which they had paid.

The owner and stage driver were fit to be tied, while everyone else ate a good meal and awaited the next development in this strange happening. After a bit, the Peddler picked up the coffeepot. "Why is this thing so heavy, do you suppose?" he asked no one in particular. He opened the lid and looked inside, then held it out for the tavern keeper to see. Inside were the silver spoons.

The Peddler smiled. "Wasn't it lucky I found them? Now we can be on our way with no further trouble."

The passengers had quite a laugh to help pass the time on their trip, the Yankee Peddler won his bet, and the stingy tavern master was madder than a raccoon stuck in a stovepipe.

WAS there really a Yankee Peddler who traveled from his home in the Eastern states to the Western territories of North America, selling needles and thread, leather polish, cod liver oil, and his own concoctions of cure-alls? Did roadside taverns serve turkey dinners? The answer to all those questions is yes. Like all folktales, fact and fancy are so intertwined they can't be separated.

Folklore is a little bit factual and a little bit made up—but is *true* in a deep and important way. It tells us something about what people really believe and how they see themselves. For instance, Davy Crockett was an excellent shot and a real hero at the Alamo, but he didn't "kill him a bear when he was only three." Still, his amazing strength and cunning give us a glimpse into the dreams and hopes of the ordinary Americans who made Davy a hero. Fact or fiction, folktales are so enjoyable and interesting, it doesn't really matter if they are not totally believable. They still tell us important things about a particular region and its people.

When the settlers came to North America they brought very few possessions with them. Life was hard; work seemed unending. The cli-

As late as the 1950s, Davy Crockett was an important folk hero for school children, who often dressed like Davy.

Even the most sober-minded North Americans have always enjoyed exaggeration. For example, Benjamin Franklin was sent by the government to London to give the British a better idea of how the new nation was getting along. He was amused by the English travelers who spent only a few weeks in America and went back home to write books—so Franklin made fun of them in his letters to the king, complaining that no mention had been made of the extraordinary sheep in America who grew so much wool they had to be harnessed to tiny carts that helped them hold the weight of their tails.

mate was different and even the trees, animals, and plants were unfamiliar. The settlers were homesick, and one way to lessen this ***nostalgia*** was to gather in each other's homes and tell stories. Of course, the stories they knew came from their home country. In time, as they felt more at home in the New World, the stories were changed and new ones were invented to reflect their surroundings and their work. Experiences that inspired these stories could be funny or tragic. The same story could be told in a brief version, or a good storyteller might add enough twists and turns to make it last an hour or more. (Remember, these people had no television to fill their evening hours.)

As the settlers spread across the continent of North America, they carried their stories and folk culture with them. Often people from a certain region of Europe, a particular ethnic background, or a particular religion would tend to all settle in the same area. Their common folklore would then shape the folklore of that region. Other times, settlers from many different ethnic

backgrounds would end up living close to one another in the same region. Although each group retained much of its traditions, they also influenced each other—and the folklore of them all was shaped by the demands and circumstances of that particular geographical region. Gradually, they came to share a common folklore.

After the United States won independence from Britain, Dr. Samuel Latham Mitchell decided that kings should no longer be mentioned in America, not even in folklore. He rewrote familiar tales and rhymes. A Mother Goose verse that originally went:

When the pie was open,
The birds began to sing.
Wasn't that a pretty dish
To set before the king?

Was changed to read:

When the pie was open,
The birds were songless.
Wasn't that a pretty dish
To set before the Congress?

No one paid any attention to Dr. Mitchell's new versions of folklore.

The stories and traditions of these regions do not belong to any one person; anyone can share a region's folklore without fear of being accused of stealing. As we enjoy the foods and festivals, jokes and songs of a particular region, we come to understand that particular area a little better. Folklore is as old as the land itself . . . and as new as today. It is constantly changing, and yet it always keeps some of its ancient flavors.

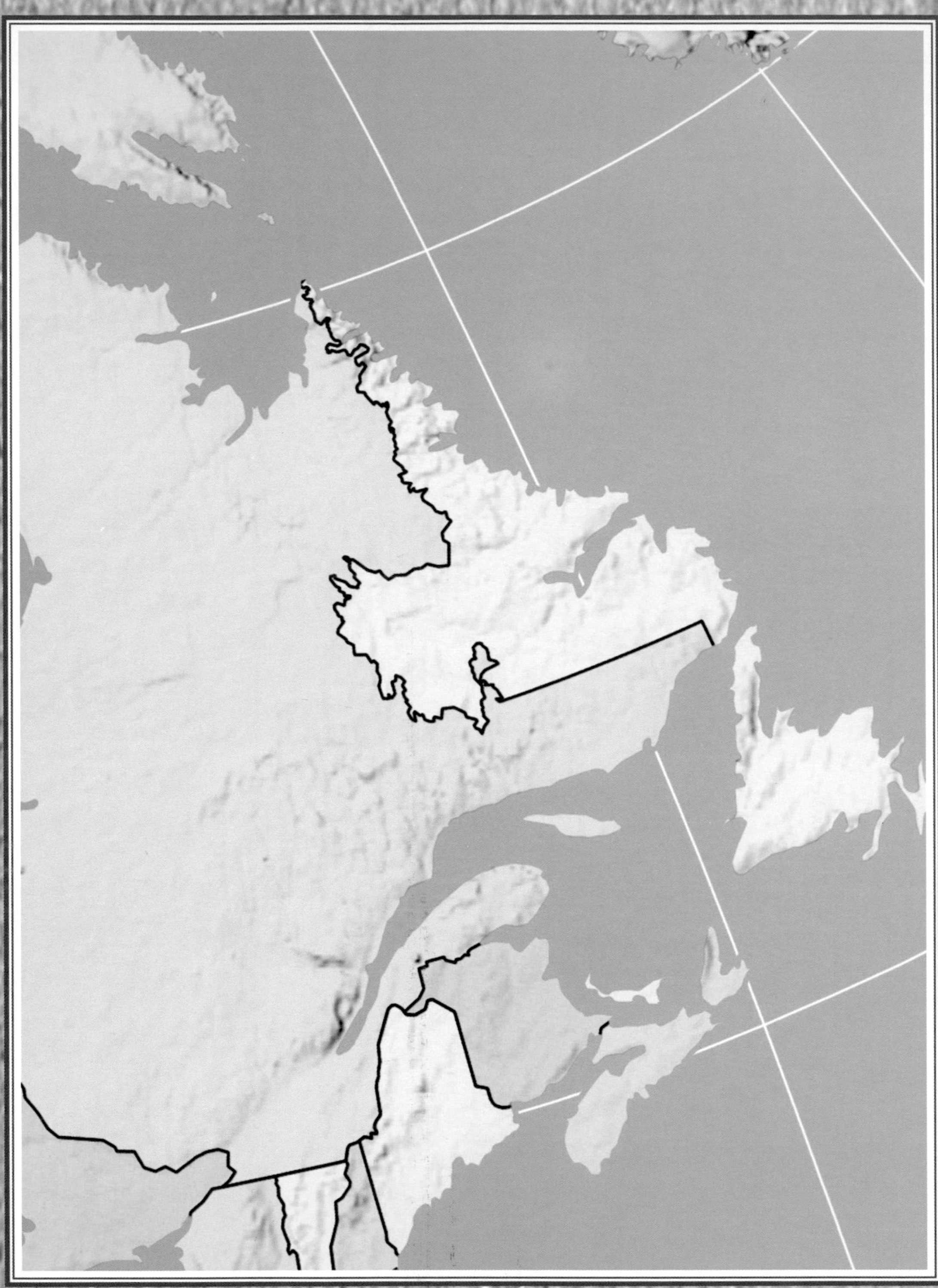

Eastern Canada.

TWO

Folklore of Eastern Canada

Dreams of Snow and Wilderness

The Inuit of northeastern Canada tell the story of the fox-bride.

IN THE DEEP northern cold of Labrador lived a lonely Inuit man whose only companions were Sun, Wind, Stars, and Snow. He left his cabin nearly every day to hunt and fish for his food and to find firewood. On those days when he had plenty of food, he cooked his meals and cleaned his cabin. If he needed a new coat, he scraped and dried animal skins and then sewed the pieces together.

The daylight had almost faded away one day when he returned home tired and hungry. With fingers so cold they were numb, he struggled with the door latch—and then, when the door finally swung open, he dropped his ice chopper on his foot from surprise.

"Yoohooee!" he yelped (or something like that; it was hard to hear him through all the fur around his hooded jacket). He hopped around the cabin on his good foot, staring in amazement at the hot supper that was waiting on the iron stove. The cabin had even been swept, he noticed. But there was no sign of the person who had done this work for him.

He was too tired to think about it very long, so he ate the supper and went to bed. The next morning he went out hunting instead of ice fishing. When he got home, he could feel warmth as soon as he opened the door. His ice axe was freshly sharpened, a hot supper was waiting, and his clean clothes were folded neatly.

From then on, every time he went out the same thing happened. Then one morning he pretended to leave, but instead, he hid nearby in order to spy on his mysterious friend. As he watched, he saw a fox slink up to the cabin. It slipped its paw into a crack in the door and pushed it open.

To help them endure the loneliness, the men had many daydreams about miraculously being able to transport themselves back to their loved ones. Perhaps they shared these fantasies with each other around the campfire to while away the long, cold hours. In any event, stories of a magical, flying canoe spread throughout the voyageurs.

ONE New Year's Eve, Pierre wanted to go home to celebrate the holiday with his family. He whispered his plan to his friend Jacques as they sat with the other men around the fireplace in their shanty.

"Are you crazy?" Jacques laughed. "It's 300 miles, a month's journey. You can't be home for a party tonight."

Pierre grinned. "Come with me. We'll go by *chasse-galerie* and be back in time for breakfast. But we'll need another five men to come with us. It takes seven to paddle the flying canoe."

At first the other men laughed, just as Jacques had, when Pierre told them his plan, but eventually he convinced them to get in the canoe. "But you can't touch a drop of alcohol at the party," he warned them.

"Sure, sure," they laughed as they picked up the oars.

Pierre whispered the magic words—and to the men's amazement, the canoe slipped out of the water, up into the air, as sweetly as a bird taking flight. The startled men began to row, and soon they were slicing through the cold

Voyageurs.

dark air, while the snow-covered hills fled backward beneath them.

"There are the lights of Montreal," one man said in an awed voice. And then, as gently as thistledown, they landed on the hillside east of the town.

Pierre's family welcomed them to their New Year's party. Pierre danced all night with his sweetheart, while the other men boasted of their adventures to the rest of the ladies. They ate and laughed—and eventually they gave in and drank more alcohol than they should.

By three o'clock in the morning, none of them were sober. It was time for them to leave, but when they rose into the air, the canoe swayed back and forth, as though it too were drunk. They zipped over the frozen land, barely skimming the trees, and zig-zagged between the steeples of Montreal, the men groaning and shouting with each swoop and dip.

Somehow they managed to make their way back to their camp, but just as they neared the shanty, Pierre stood up to wave with his paddle, hoping to get the attention of the other men on the ground below. Everyone knows you can't stand up in a canoe; the magic vessel capsized, and the men found themselves falling down through the snowy branches of a fir tree. Their companions later discovered them unhurt in a snowdrift. No one believed the story they told of their magical adventures—but it made a good tale to tell around the fire.

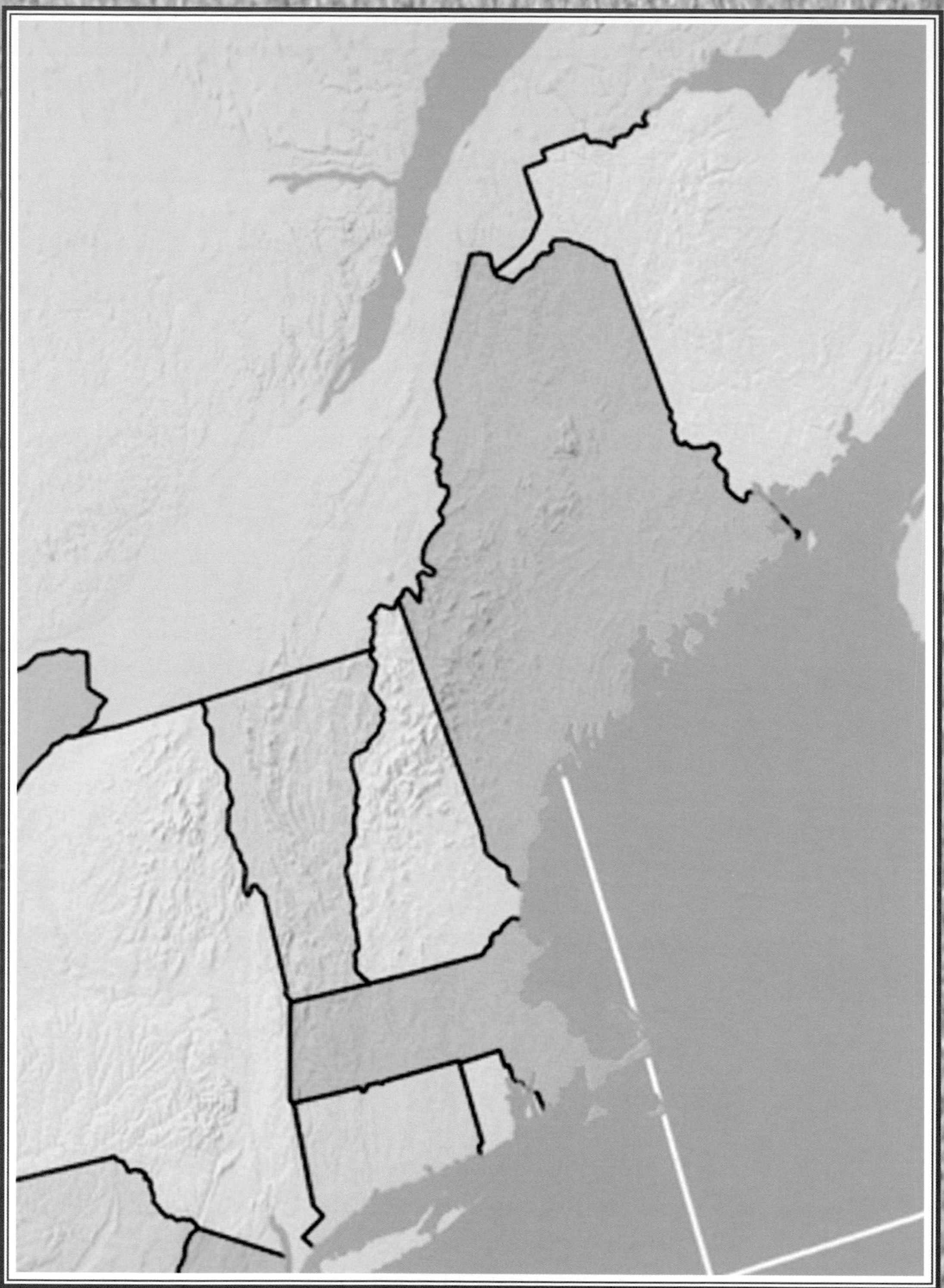

The New England states.

THREE

New England Folklore

Ghost Ships and Witchcraft

Tales of ghost ships are common in New England.

LIKE AN OLD coin that has passed through many hands, a folktale picks up a little of each person who tells it. Although we may be able to trace a particular story to one or several sources, ultimately, no one can claim ownership of these timeless stories. They slip through our hands like seawater.

IN 1647 a Rhode Island–built ship carrying a valuable cargo of trade goods and about 20 passengers departed from New Haven, Connecticut, bound for England. The ship was new, but the master, a Captain Lamberton, did not like the way she handled. She wallowed in the water and seemed heavy and awkward. With a cold shudder, Lamberton admitted to himself that he feared she would be the grave of her passengers and crew.

Their journey began in the cold, dead heart of winter; the harbor was partly frozen, and a way had to be broken through the ice as the ship set sail. As Lamberton's ship disappeared over the horizon, a minister on shore led the townspeople in common prayer: "Lord, if it be your pleasure to bury our friends at the bottom of the sea, take them; save them."

Winter eventually melted into spring, but the ships arriving from England brought no news of Captain Lamberton's vessel or his passengers. The people of New Haven tried to keep their hopes up, but feared the worst.

One afternoon in June of that year, a great thunderstorm rose out of the northwest. After it passed, the skies cleared and the sun shone. Then, about an hour before sunset, the people saw a large ship, all sails spread to the wind and flags flying in the breeze. As the townspeople watched, a hush fell over them.

The wind was still out of the northwest, dead against the ship, and yet she still moved steadily toward shore, as though her sails were filled with a favorable stiff breeze from the east. The strange ship seemed to float on air, leaving not a ripple or wave on the calm sea. No hands were on deck busying themselves to make anchor; no passengers stood against the sky straining for their first sight of land; and no one was at the tiller.

When the ship had sailed as far in as such a ship could without running aground, a man at last appeared on the forward deck. He drew his sword and pointed seaward. Suddenly, the ship behaved as though caught in a terrible storm. The mainmast broke, and the sails all hung in a tangle. Then the spars, masts, and sails blew away in this strange phantom wind, leaving a hulk that careened wildly in the harbor, keeled over, and then slipped under the surface of the water in a gray mist.

The Specter Ship was believed to have been sent to show the people of New Haven what had happened. Now they could stop watching and waiting for news. Their friends and loved ones had been lost at sea in a howling winter storm.

THIS eerie story was reported as a real event, witnessed by an entire town full of people. And yet it contains elements of other ghost stories at sea. It's as though people around the world, but especially in a particular region, are all dreaming the same dreams.

In Maine it was believed that if you pointed at a daffodil with your index finger it would not bloom.

Witches were thought to have power over animals and the weather.

Ships and the sea would have been important elements in the dreams of New Englanders. The rocky land was difficult to farm, and early settlers clung to the coast, creating fishing and seafaring communities. The sea's rhythms ruled their lives and shaped their folklore.

The Old World was another influence on New England folklore. The early New Englanders came to North America to start over—but they couldn't help bringing with them the traditions and beliefs of England, the land from which many of them came. Superstitions like lucky horseshoes, breaking the wishbone for good luck, love charms, interpretation of dreams, and fear of the number 13 all crossed the Atlantic to New England. The Old World's fear of witches and demons also slunk across the ocean, with tragic results.

The Salem witch trials began as a reaction to the unexplained torment of two young girls in Salem Village. Because no physical evidence could be found for their behavior, it was concluded Satan was tormenting them. Forced to reveal the witches who had afflicted them, the girls named three women, only the first of the

These fishermen are "buying wind" from a sorcerer. He will give it to them in the knotted rope.

Fishermen and other seafarers from New England faced a dangerous and uncertain life. Perhaps to give themselves a greater sense of control, they developed superstitions based on avoiding bad luck at sea. Here are a few:

Never turn around to get something you've forgotten once you've headed out to sea.

If you have to turn a boat against the sun, go home and put her in her mooring or you'll have bad luck all day.

Always launch new ships wet—never launch them dry. (In other words, to avoid bad luck, have a big launching party with plenty to drink.)

Never bring a black suitcase on board a boat.

If you turn the ***hatch*** bottom up, you'll end up at the bottom of the sea.

Never "buy the wind" (throw a coin into the water while asking God to send wind), because the Lord is liable to send a hurricane.

many women and few men from various standings in the community who would eventually be accused of practicing witchcraft.

Before the ***hysteria*** ended, 24 individuals were killed. In this case, the region's folklore was destructive. Folklore often provides reasons for unexplained events, offering people comfort and a greater sense of control over reality's terrors—but in Massachusetts in the 17th century, this folklore led people to believe their fellow townspeople were actually ***emissaries*** of Satan.

According to folklore, witches were created when the Devil "baptized" his followers.

Today, tales of witchcraft and evil are still prevalent in New England folklore. For instance, in 20th-century Maine, many families still passed along stories of a powerful and malicious local witch who older members of the family claimed to remember. Stories continued to grow even after the old woman's death, as people were said to "call up her spirit."

Not all of New England's folklore is ghostly and goose-bumpy of course. New Englanders also love to tell jokes, particularly "Irishman" stories such as the one that follows.

In New England, "forerunners" are thought to be omens of approaching death. The forerunner is often the ghostly image of a previously deceased family member.

Two men were in a boat when the boat flipped over and they both fell into the water. The Irishman started swimming toward shore, but the other man couldn't swim, so he just

In the area around Boston there is a type of rock called pudding stone. This very unscientific name was given to it because marble-size pebbles are imbedded in the conglomerate that forms the larger rock.

Local folklore tells of a giant who had an unpleasant wife and three unruly children. The giant put the children in a playpen and brought them a pudding stuffed with plums. Puddings in those days were more like a soft fruitcake and this one was as big as the dome on the state capital.

As soon as the father left for work, those three giant kids had a food fight in their playpen. They yelled and threw handfuls of plum pudding around. The lumps of pudding hardened and are seen around Boston to this day as pudding stones.

floundered around and shouted for help. A crowd gathered on the shore, and they too shouted: "Save that man! He can't swim." But the Irishman paid no attention to any of them; he just kept swimming. When he finally staggered on shore, the crowd demanded to know why he wouldn't help the other man. "Why,"

Weather folklore was important to New England sailors. Observing the natural world gave them important clues that could save a ship or even a life.

Red sky at night, sailors delight.
Red sky at morning, sailors take warning.

When the leaves on trees turn over it foretells wind and possibly severe weather.

FESTIVALS IN THE NEW ENGLAND STATES

Connecticut Storytelling Festival—New London, Connecticut
Keepers of the Lore—Joseph, Vermont
Campbell Festival of Myth, Folklore, and Storytelling—Milford, New Hampshire
Champlain Valley Folk Festival—Ferrisburgh

the Irishman replied, "I had to save myself first. Now I'll go back and get the poor sod."

THESE stories reflect regional prejudice, since they imply that Irishmen are not quite so sensible as other New Englanders. In modern New England, however, stories like these are the echoes of long-ago prejudice that has in most cases ceased to divide the region's population.

The Mid-Atlantic states.

FOUR

Folklore of the Mid-Atlantic States

Hoop Snakes, Headless Horsemen, and Jersey Devils

Stories of pirates were common along the Atlantic coast.

THE PENNSYLVANIA hoop snake is a strange being. It is long and multi-colored, and the poison stinger in its tail is something to be reckoned with. You can tell a hoop snake from an everyday snake by the way it moves: a hoop snake travels by grabbing the end of its tail in its mouth and rolling along until it comes up to something to sting.

Well, Abner was hoeing his field one day when a hoop snake came rolling up to him. He figured he was a goner, but the snake missed and stung the hoe handle instead. The poison stinger stuck in the hoe, and Abner ran off. He had to wait until dark anyhow to get his hoe. (Everyone knows hoop snakes that get into fights don't die until sundown.)

Sure enough, at sundown the snake was cold dead, but the hoe handle was all swollen up from the poison. It was so swollen, Abner took it to a sawmill and had lumber made from it for a new chicken coop.

THIS folktale may give us a taste of the Mid-Atlantic states' regional personality—but in fact, each state has its own unique flavors, due to its history and the country of origin of its settlers.

For instance, in Pennsylvania, the "Dutch," including Amish and Mennonite folk, are very strict about following the customs and beliefs of their religion. But they are not without humor, and they are not Dutch. The word in the German language for German is *Deutsch*, which was mispronounced by the English settlers as Dutch.

The Amish live a very simple life without modern conven-

The hoop snake.

iences. They have more children than the average American family does, because parents need helpers for their many household and farm chores. The hoop snake tale is still told to unsuspecting young children by older siblings who had the joke played on them when they first went to the vegetable garden to hoe weeds.

Meanwhile, to the north of Pennsylvania, in New York State, some of the region's most famous tales are the products of both folklore and literature. The Catskill Mountains gave birth to the spooky story of the *Legend of Sleepy Hollow* with its Headless Horseman, and Washington Irving wrote the story as literature, based on both the folklore and the politics of the time.

Belief in tommyknockers came from the miners who emigrated from Cornwall, England. The tap-tap sounds were made by the mischievous elfin creatures who would steal from lunch pails and hide hand tools. Miners believed these gnomes would watch over them and warn them of danger. In return, miners left a bit of their lunch on the ground to stay on the tommyknockers' good side. (Actually, the tapping sounds were probably made by the support timbers shifting just before a collapse.) Miners also believed tommyknockers did not like whistling or swearing.

The Pennsylvania Dutch also have their own folk medicine. According to one tradition, various illnesses are caused by the blood moving too fast through the body's vessels. Healers (called powwowers) have spells for stilling the blood, a cure that can be accomplished even over the phone. One healer uses this charm:

Three roses stood on the Lord Jesus' grave.
The one was named humility,
The other was named gentleness,
And the third was named God's will.
So shall the blood of [the patient's name] be still.

The coalmines of Pennsylvania, Virginia, and West Virginia have a wealth of superstitious folklore. For instance:

- Women in a mine were thought to be bad luck.
- If a miner's headlamp went out it meant his wife or girlfriend was cheating on him.
- Miners liked to sit in the same seat on the tram on the way into and out of the mine, and to eat lunch in the same spot, as a way of ensuring predictability in their workday. (For a miner, predictability and good luck are the same thing!)

Washington Irving also used the folktale of Rip Van Winkle, the lazy and hen-pecked fellow who went to sleep up in the mountains for 20 years. When he returned home, things had changed. He no longer knew the people, familiar shops were gone, and his favorite tavern no longer had a carving of the king on the sign. Instead, George Washington was featured. The story of Rip Van Winkle was originally a German fairy tale, adapted by Irving to portray the awakening of the new country to new leaders and renewed energy.

The Amish like to play practical jokes, as is clear in this anecdote:

A boy asks a farmer, "If I pick the cherries from this tree can I have half?" The farmer agrees and the boy picks the fruit and is ready to leave. "Where is my half?" asks the farmer. "Yet on the tree," says the lad. "I only asked for half."

A little further south, little New Jersey has tried to get some respect from the earliest times of the colonies. The birth of the Jersey Devil at least gave the residents something unique that historic Pennsylvania and wealthy New York did not have.

Hog Wallow, Double Trouble, and Ongs Hat are just a few of the strange names of tiny villages and ghostly ruins in the remote part of southern New Jersey called the Pine Barrens. The sandy

The Headless Horseman was a folktale that gave goose bumps to children in colonial New York—but Washington Irving used the old story as a way of saying to adults that a man without a head may seem frightening, but if you think about it, he no longer has a brain and should not be feared. The horseman was a symbol for the king who had lost his power over the colonies.

Captain Kidd is said to have buried some treasure on Raritan Bay, New Jersey.

FESTIVALS IN THE MID-ATLANTIC STATES

Groundhog Day with Punxsutawney Phil—Punxsutawney, Pennsylvania
Chincoteague Island Storyfest (tales of wild horses and legends of the sea)—
Chincoteague Island, Virginia
Falcon Ridge Folk Festival—Hillsdale, New York
New Jersey Folk Festival at Rutgers University—New Brunswick, New Jersey

soil and cedar-stained water in the marshy streams make the land all but unfit for growing crops. (However, cranberries and blueberries thrive here, and they are two of the area's major crops.) The trees are stunted, giving the landscape an eerie appearance.

It is rumored that the pirate Captain Kidd buried some treasure nearby on Raritan Bay in 1700. When Kidd was arrested for piracy, he claimed to have hidden a treasure worth 40,000 British pounds. If he was released, he promised he would give the treasure to the government. The court did not listen to his pleas, however, and he took the secret of his treasure with him to his grave. Today treasure seekers still search for Captain Kidd's gold—and some claim to have seen his ghost. The pirate is said to still sail the waters off New Jersey's coast, seeking his hidden treasure.

But Captain Kidd is nothing compared to the Jersey Devil.

IN 1735, a woman in the Pine Barrens had her 13th baby. Some say she cursed it for being born because she already had 12 children. Others say she was a witch. In any event, as soon as the child was born, it began to grow and change. Within minutes, it was a beast with a head like a horse, a bat's wings, and a lizard-like body with a long forked tail. Instead of crying like a normal newborn, it made horrible screaming and hissing noises. It was taller than a man and strong enough to beat the nurse with its tail.

This horrible creature has haunted the Pine Barrens of southern New Jersey ever since. Descriptions vary so much it was conveniently decided that the thing could change size and appearance. Some claim he does his worst every seven years, but the schedule varies. Apparently, he stalks the land just before wars. He is blamed for crop failures, droughts, hurricane winds, and cows not producing milk. Fish die in large numbers

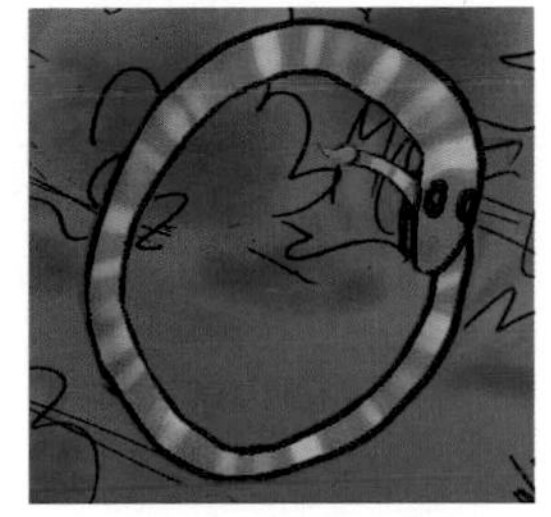

when he boils the streams with his fiery breath.

Some residents of the Pine Barrens today say the Devil doesn't exist . . . but they are still a little nervous about walking the sandy trails alone. Just as the Pennsylvanians taught their children to fear the hoop snake, those of the Pine Barrens warn their children and others about wandering alone in the dark.

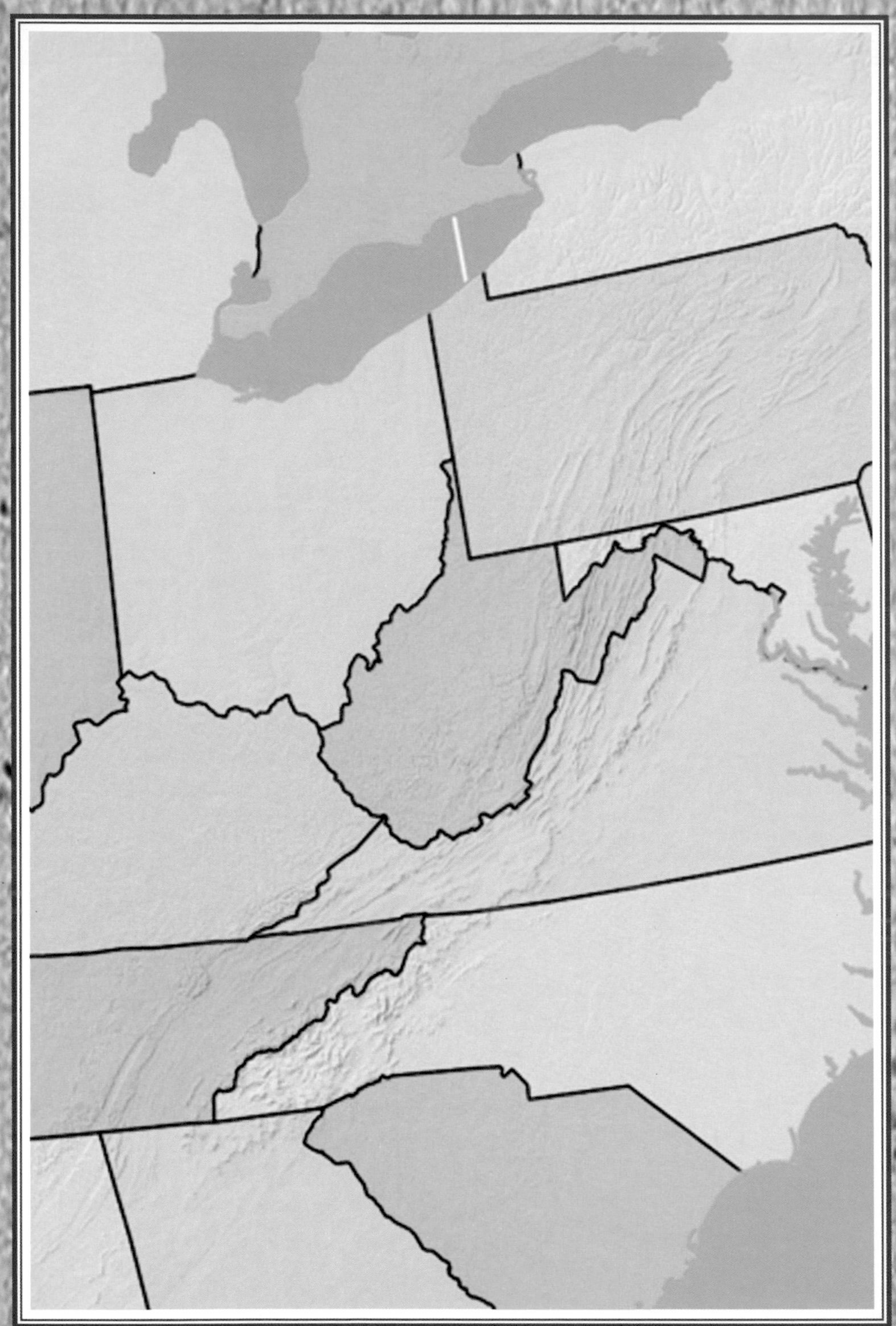

The Appalachian region.

FIVE

Appalachian Mountain Folklore

Woodsmen, Catfish, Murder, and Song

Davy Crockett was credited with many amazing feats.

ONCE UPON A time the mountainous parts of western Virginia, West Virginia, North Carolina, Tennessee, and Kentucky were the ***frontier***. Woodsmen like Daniel Boone and Davy Crockett set out from their homes in the Appalachians to explore the west. Folks were pretty sure Davy Crockett was someone special even before he saved the whole earth.

One night when Davy was headed home from a night of bear hunting, it was so cold the dawn had frozen solid. The sun was caught between two blocks of ice and the earth had iced up and stopped turning. Davy was a smart man and knew he had to do something quick or everything in the world would die. The bear he had over his shoulder was a fresh kill and the carcass was still warm, so he climbed up on the jagged, frozen sunbeams until he reached the sun. He wrapped that warm bear around the ice blocks until they melted, then gave the sun a good kick to get it spinning again. He put the bear on his back, slid down the sunrays before they thawed out, and went home for breakfast.

In the hollows (called hollers) of the Great Smokies and Blue Ridge Mountains there are still settlements where people retell tall tales like this one. Many of these people make their own clothes, build their own houses, grow their own food, hunt, and fish much as they have done for more than 200 years.

These people of the Appalachian region are fiercely independent of outsiders and very protective of their own families, neighbors, and folklore. In very few other areas of North America will you find as much folk culture being lived as part of the daily lives of the people. Other regions may have living museums and

APPALACHIAN HUNTING AND FISHING SUPERSTITIONS

According to the fishermen in the mountains, fish bite best at night, and if you play a fiddle or guitar the fish just can't stay in the water but will come to the top because they love the music.

If you are out hunting and see your shadow, it is a sign that you will not get any game that day.

Wrap a black horsehair around your wrist and you will shoot straight.

If you go fishing and play the harmonica, all the snakes will come around.

reconstructed pioneer forts to show tourists what life was like 100 to 200 years ago, but there are "hollers" in the eastern mountains that have changed little since Davy's day.

"Dropping in" is a common practice there. Some modern conveniences have come to the mountains, but not everyone can afford a telephone, and neighbors may be a mile or more away. When a family can take a break from work, especially on a weekend, they may take some vegetables or eggs as a gift and drop in on a neighbor, "set a spell," comparing folk remedies or telling stories. The children still love to here the elders tell these tales.

OLD Charley went fishing at his favorite spot and caught a mess of catfish. Once he got home, he put them on a stringer and started to clean them.

As Charley tells it, "One big catfish was still breathing, so I tossed him over in the grass and forgot about him until after supper. Well, that fish was *still* breathing, so I got an idea. I fixed him a bucket of water, and next day I took him out for two hours. Next day I took him out for three hours and pretty soon he could stay out of water nearly all day.

"I named him Jethro and he was the best pet. I put a little string around him and took him with me everywhere I'd go. He'd wiggle along through the grass and gravel, down the road. He'd follow me to town even when I tried to chase him back home. Well, one day I crossed the wooden bridge over the creek—the one with the rotted, broken board in the middle—and when I

Davy Crockett's backwoods life became a North American tradition.

APPALACHIAN CHRISTMAS CAROL

The Cherry Tree Carol

Joseph and Mary
Were a-walking one fine day,
"Here are apples and cherries
Pretty to behold."

Then Mary said to Joseph
So meek and so mild,
"Joseph, pick me cherries,
For I am with child."

Then Joseph he got angry,
In anger all he flew,
"Let the father of your baby
Pick cherries for you."

Then the babe it spoke a few words,
A few words to the tree,
Let my mother have some cherries,
Bow down, you cherry tree."

The cherry tree bowed low down,
Bowed down to the ground,
And Mary she ate cherries,
While Joseph stood around.

Then Joseph took Mary
On his knee,
"Oh tell of your baby,
When will his birthday be?"

"On the sixth of January,"
The babe said softly,
"On the sixth of January
My birthday will be."

WEATHER SUPERSTITIONS

Ants are busy, gnats bite, crickets sing louder, spiders come down from their webs, and flies gather in houses just before rain.

If the sky turns green during a storm, there will be hail.

looked back, Jethro was nowhere to be seen. I looked down and there was Jethro in the creek. Before I could get to him, he drowned."

THIS story reflects the love of exaggeration and preposterous events that is common to much of North American folklore. But the Appalachian region also has many other, still older stories to offer. These are tales of murder and witchcraft, magic and

APPALACHIAN FOLK CURES

If you have a high fever and are past 14 years old, put eight drops of turpentine on one half teaspoonful of sugar and take that for three mornings.

To secure a good remedy for fever or measles, ask for one from a stranger on horseback; if the stranger is riding a white horse, the remedy will be more effective.

FESTIVALS IN THE APPALACHIANS

Haunting in the Hills Storytelling Festival—National Park Service at Big South Fork National River and Recreation Area, Tennessee
National Storytelling Festival—Jonesborough, Tennessee
Appalachian String Band Music Festival—Clifftop, West Virginia
Appalachian Heritage Festival—Sheperdstown, West Virginia
Oldtime Fiddlers' Convention—Galax, Virginia

wonder. Some of them are dark and gruesome—like the story of the crying stairwell, where the tiny skeletons of five murdered babies were found hidden beneath the stair boards. And then there's the tale of Old Foster, a man who caught women, boiled them, and ate them. Lurid stories like these make the *National Inquirer* look tame by comparison.

The original tales told in the Appalachians were brought there by those who came from Great Britain and elsewhere, looking for a way to support their families. Because the Appalachians were rich with minerals, many men turned to mining—gold, iron, silver, lead, and copper. In addition to the mines, roads and railroads needed to be built in this rough terrain and it took many strong men. John Henry was a real person who drove the steel spikes that held the rails to the ties. Did this "steel drivin'" man die while trying to beat a steam machine brought in to replace the men who did this job? The song says it is so, and we know the invention of machinery in the late 1800s put many men with families and homes out of work.

The Appalachian region has a rich musical heritage as well. Much of today's country music has its roots in Appalachia, and bluegrass music was born here. This unique culture is apparently fertile ground for all manner of folk creativity.

Poverty and simplicity are facts of life in the Appalachian region. But the people who live there are connected to the land and to each other—and to the past, a past rich with tales and songs of survival and families, tragedy and humor.

In the golden days of railroad, crews of men laid rails and dug tunnels by hand. John Henry worked for the C&O railroad. He was renowned for his strength and skill in driving steel rods into the rock for inserting dynamite. His partner held the long steel drill and turned it by hand as John Henry swung a big hammer, driving the rod into the rock, drilling the Big Bend Tunnel in Greenbrier County, West Virginia.

The steam drill was invented around 1870, and the crew at the other end of the Big Bend Tunnel used one. There was a lot of ribbing and boasting between the two companies as to who could dig faster. A hundred-dollar reward was offered in a contest over who could drill faster, and John Henry took the bet. At the end of the day the steam drill drilled through nine feet of rock, and John Henry drilled 12. He won the prize but died that night from the exertion. For years afterward people claimed they heard the sound of hammering in the mountain.

When John Henry was a little baby,
Sitting on his Mammy's knee,
Said the Big Bend Tunnel on that C and O Road,
"Gonna be the death of me,
Gonna be the death of me."

Well, the captain said to John Henry,
"Gonna bring that steam drill round.
Gonna bring that steam drill out on the job,
Gonna whup that steel on down,
Gonna whup that steel on down."

John Henry said to the Captain,
"A man ain't nothin' but a man.
But before I let a steam drill beat me down,
I'll die with a hammer in my hand,
I'll die with a hammer in my hand."

John Henry said to the captain,
"I'm gonna take a little trip downtown,
Get me a 30-pound hammer with that nine-foot handle
I'll beat your steam drill down,
I'll beat your steam drill down."

Now the man that invented the steam drill,
He thought he was mighty fine.
But John Henry drove 15 feet,
The steam drill made only nine,
The steam drill made only nine.

John hammered on the mountain,
Till his hammer was striking fire,
But he swung so hard he broke his heart,
And he laid down his hammer and he died,
He laid down his hammer and he died.

They took John Henry to the graveyard,
Laid him down in the sand,
And every time a locomotive goes rolling on by,
They say, "There lies a steel drivin' man,
There lies a steel drivin' man."

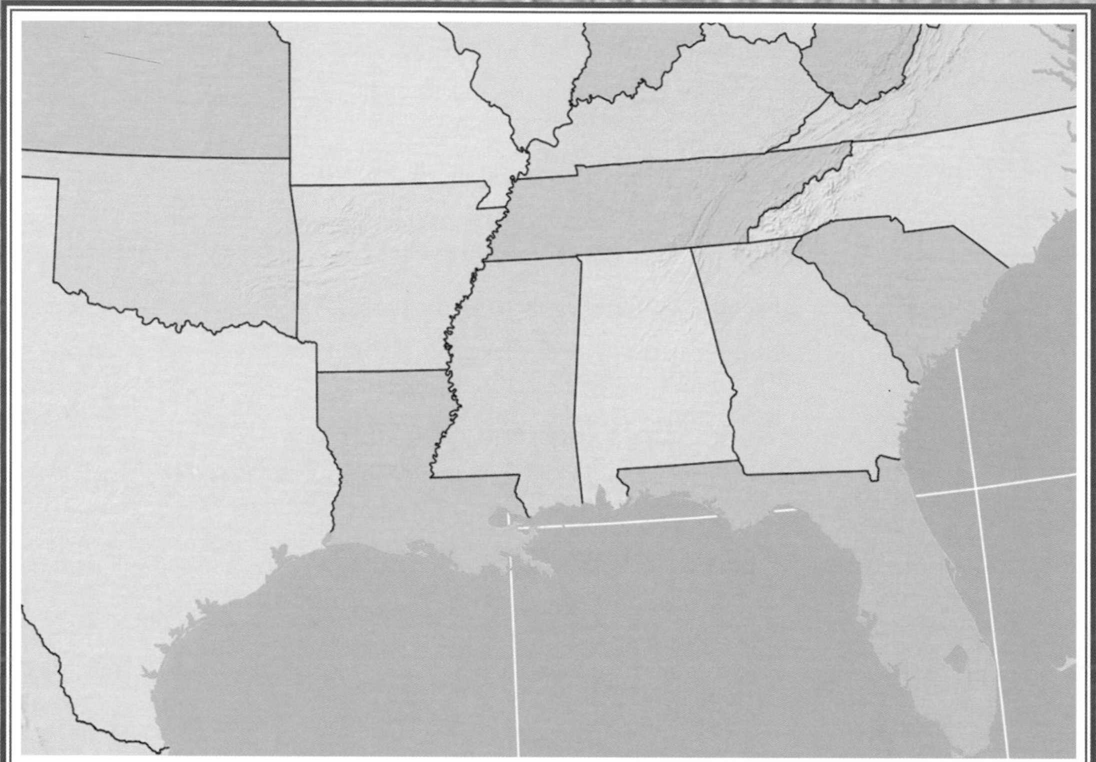

The Southern states.

SIX

Folklore of the South

Imagination and Family

Stories of Bre'r Rabbit—or Compère Lapin, as he is known in Louisiana—are common in the South.

LISTENING TO A folktale told by a Southerner is a delightful experience. The flavor and rhythm of the language of the rural Deep South, mixed with African and French words, cannot be mistaken for any other region of North America.

Even after the end of slavery in the 1860s, many folks lacked the ability to read and write, and the oral tradition of folklore was stronger here than in the north. (The high rate of illiteracy was due to lack of educational opportunities, not lack of intelligence.) The slaves and the poor white ***sharecroppers*** used the power of imagination to ease the hardship of their lives, telling and retelling folktales of brave and cunning heroes.

One such trickster, Br'er Rabbit, is well known to children throughout the United States, although he originated in Africa. This tricky bunny came to North America with the slaves, and his stories were translated into French by the Creoles, or French-speaking blacks, and the Cajuns, French people who came from the part of Nova Scotia called Acadia and settled in Louisiana. It was here that our rabbit friend came to be known as Compère Lapin (Comrade Rabbit).

COMPÈRE Lapin loved to torment Alligator. Once Alligator's skin was white and smooth and he took his naps in the shade with Spanish moss for a pillow. One day Compère Lapin tippy-toed up on Alligator's back without waking him and drizzled sorghum syrup between the gator's tender toes and on his head. Well, don't you know every wasp and ant and fly in the

parish showed up like a Sunday picnic and commenced biting poor Alligator.

"Help, Lapin!" cried Alligator. "They're eating me alive!"

But Lapin was rolling on the ground holding his belly from laughing so hard.

Compère Alligator couldn't take all that meanness the bugs were delivering to his tender toes. He jumped straight up in the air, thwacked his head on a tree limb, and crashed back to earth so hard sparks flew from his feet and set the grass on fire. Alligator danced like he was doing a Cajun two-step, then took a flying leap into the ***bayou***, landing with a hiss and a sizzle. He cooled down, but his hide was as blistered and bumpy as the bark of a cypress, just as it is today.

GHOST SOLDIERS

The Civil War was more costly to the Confederate southern states than to the northern Union. The loss of life was terrible on both sides, but the South suffered greater economic losses and a change in their way of life. There are many ghostly folktales about the conflict. For instance, in Charleston, South Carolina, people claim to hear horses' hooves, the low voices of men, and the rattle of wagons and cannons rolling down the streets at midnight. If they look out their windows, they say there is a gray mist, and it is just possible to make out the shadowy outlines of the Army of the Dead.

FESTIVALS IN THE SOUTH

The Kentucky Festival of the Arts—Northport, near Tuscaloosa, Alabama
Louisiana Folklife Festival—Monroe, Louisiana
Florida Folk Festival—Stephen Foster Folk Culture Center State Park, White Springs on the Suwannee River, White Springs, Florida
Swamp Gravy Storytelling Festival—Colquitt, Georgia
Tidewater Traditional Arts Festival—Hampton, Virginia

STORIES like these may illustrate their tellers' longing to be in control of their own lives, to overcome their lot in life through cleverness and trickery.

Imagination may have helped to lighten the heavy loads they carried, but so did the close bonds they forged between family members. Family life is still very important in the South. Married children tend to live close to their parents and siblings. This results in several generations of grandparents, great aunts, cousins, uncles, and all the other relatives getting together often for family picnics, celebrations, or the barbeques that are so popular in the South. Kinfolk know each other very well and a good bit of teasing, storytelling, and playing of practical jokes are features of these family gatherings. Almost every tale is told as a true account of a happening to one relative or another. As long as the storyteller sounds sincere, the listeners have a hard time separating fact from fiction. The tales are passed around for years, details and names changing to fit the occasion.

UNCLE Harold used to make charcoal in Georgia. (You make charcoal in a big ***kiln*** with dry wood stacked in it a special way so it gets hot but the wood doesn't burn to ashes. Some kilns are built into a hillside and are bigger than a room in a house.)

To light the kiln, Uncle Harold would fill it with wood and then use a 20-foot iron pole with a kerosene rag on the end of it. The flame on the end of the pole would reach all the way to the back of the kiln, and he could tell when the wood caught fire.

Once my little cousin Kenny asked Uncle how he lit it, and Uncle said he hired a boy to crawl way back there and light it.

"Aren't you afraid he'll get hung up?" Kenny asked.

"No." Uncle replied. "I tie a rope to him and if he gets hung up I pull him out."

"How much do you pay him?" Kenny was serious.

"Five dollars."

"Cash? Every time he comes out?"

"Yep," said Uncle Harold.

"Can I have the job? I need money for a baseball mitt."

WHY THERE ARE SO MANY HURRICANES IN THE SOUTH

The devil knew that God walked around Florida on Christmas Day, so he jumped out from behind some shrubbery and asked for a Christmas gift. Being a Southern gentleman on that day, God said he'd give the devil the east coast of Florida. The devil has been playing around with hurricanes on the east coast ever since.

According to legend, Mississippi mosquitoes are so big that two of them can pick up a man and carry him back to the swamp to share him with the whole mosquito clan.

Uncle Harold thought a bit. "No. Not this year. I have a contract for this year with another boy."

We don't know how long it was before Kenny figured out Uncle Harold was fooling him.

ONE has to wonder if the heat of the South played as important a role in the folklore as any other influences. That warm weather must surely have helped create the laid-back attitude where storytelling thrives. Life is a little slower there than in the brisk, busy North. At any rate, the combination of family traditions, African and French heritage, American history, and the environment has definitely added a richness to the lore that is all its own.

The Western region of North America.

SEVEN

Folklore of the West

Gold Mines and Gunslingers

Calamity Jane became a Western folk hero.

SOME FOLK legends may be based on historical stories. They may be true, or parts may be true. The storyteller believes them to be true, even when he passes them on with added details of his own invention.

The Cimarron Trail, the Oregon Trail, the Santa Fe Trail, the Butterfield stage route—all these existed long before settlers set foot on North America. Herds of wild horses, antelope and buffalo wore these paths into the earth. Settlers followed and named the trails. Some risked the journey west because of the government's promise of free land. Other ambitious men left their eastern farms and work, drawn by the lure of riches in the gold fields.

For each man who became rich, hundreds found just enough gold to make a living, and thousands found nothing. One of the lucky ones left a story of hidden gold as his legacy. It was called the "Lost Dutchman Mine," and many men have followed the Dutchman to the grave because of it.

The Superstition Mountains of Arizona are home to the mine originally worked by a Mexican family in the 1840s. They were the only ones who knew the location of this rich gold deposit. When the Peralta family was killed, several maps surfaced but always seemed to get misplaced. Men who claimed to have found the mine couldn't return to it or some disaster struck before they could file a claim.

In the 1870s, Jacob Waltz, "the Dutchman" (who was actually German) was said to have located the mine. He had a partner, Jacob Weiser, and the two claimed to have hidden the gold they had taken from the mine in the Superstitions. Weiser was killed, some say by Apaches, some say by Waltz, after the two men had spent more than ten years living in the area, paying their way with gold.

Jacob Waltz died in 1891 without revealing the location of the gold mine, which then became known as the "Lost Dutchman." According to legend, countless people have died trying to find the riches of the mine. Some people just disappeared; others may have left the area secretly in disappointment. The bodies of two young soldiers who had found some of the gold were discovered in the desert in 1880. Boulders have mysteriously fallen off the cliffs, injuring people. In 1927, a woman was found shot dead with several gold nuggets near her body. Two men went mad in 1910 after exploring the area of the mine. Hikers disappeared in 1956; others have fallen or have been wounded by gunshots.

Although many of these unfortunate happenings can be explained as careless accidents or the risks of hiking and camping in the desert, some defy explanation. The local residents prefer to keep alive the legend of the curse that follows all those who search for the Lost Dutchman mine.

Movies and television depict Western mining towns as wild, lawless, immoral places. Some fit this description when the first ***prospectors*** arrived, but those areas settled around rich veins of copper, silver, gold, lead, and other minerals and gems had churches, family homes, and a schoolhouse.

ALONG with the stories of mines and miners, the west was full of characters whose names are still well known. History tells us about Jesse James, Billy the Kid, Belle Starr,

Calamity Jane left home as a teenager to make her way in the world. It is hard to separate fact from fiction about this woman, since she exaggerated and told many untruths to those writing her biography. She claimed to have been married to Wild Bill Hickok. Wild Bill claimed never to have met Calamity. Calamity had the last word, though, as Wild Bill died first and Calamity arranged to be buried next to him.

Judge Roy Bean, and other brave lawmen and ruthless outlaws. These same folks also show up in tall tales and legends.

Calamity Jane was a real woman known for telling her life story the way she wanted it to be instead of the way it was. She loved attention, and if she couldn't get it by deeds, she invented a story. An orphan at age 16, she made her own way in the world. She could ride, shoot, and crack a bullwhip as well as any man. She had a crush on Wild Bill Hickok, and even though the two had never met, Calamity referred to him as her good friend. Calamity Jane became a folk hero, as legendary as the giant Paul Bunyan for all that she was a real person.

The West was truly wide open and wild, with train robberies, cattle rustling, and gun battles continuing into the early years of the 20th century. But even outlaws had their good days, according to this humorous tale.

ONE day Jesse James and his gang stopped at a farmhouse for something to eat. A

Calamity Jane's grave.

If you are a citizen of the United States, you can legally search for the Lost Dutchman mine. If you decide to do so, do not buy any maps, since there are no known maps of the Peralta mine in this country or in Mexico. Do not go alone. Be prepared for rough desert conditions. Shoot only to protect your life.

widow lived there with her children. She didn't have much, but shared what she had with the men. While they were eating, Jesse noticed that the woman had been crying and asked what was wrong. She said her mortgage was overdue and the landlord was going to put her out. She didn't know how she and her children would survive.

"How much is the mortgage?" asked Jesse James.

WANTED: YOUNG SKINNY WIRY FELLOWS not over eighteen. Must be expert riders willing to risk death daily. Orphans preferred. WAGES $25 per week. Apply, Central Overland Express, Montgomery Street (newspaper ad for Pony Express Riders)

The Pony Express carried mail and important news from the Missouri River to California under hair-raising conditions. It was the fastest link between the East and California in the years leading up to the Civil War. The Pony Express was in service only a year and a half before telegraph lines crossed the continent and made it unnecessary—and yet it earned a permanent place in the folklore of the West.

FESTIVALS IN THE WESTERN STATES

Payson Fiddlers Contest—Payson, Arizona
General Sam Houston Folk Festival—George Ranch Historical Park, Richmond, Texas
The Boulder City Folk Festival—Boulder City, Nevada
Bay Area Storytelling Festival—San Francisco, California

"Fifteen hundred dollars," replied the widow.

Jesse took out his moneybag and counted out the money for the widow.

"I can't take this," she protested but Jesse insisted and told her to be sure to get a proper receipt. She promised.

After Jesse and his men left the widow, they hid nearby. The landlord collected the money from the widow, wrote out a receipt, and rode off. He didn't get far down the trail before Jesse stole his money back.

IT took some mighty daring folks to settle the West. Most were as ordinary as the family down the street, but within every

The legends of the West are some of North America's most well-known folklore.

region special heroes evolved. In the West, these bigger-than-life men and women carried guns and rode horses. They lived beneath the stars and brandished their own sort of order, not always the same as that of the law-abiding folks. The sheer daring of these heroes and villains inspired ordinary people; it kept the average person hopeful that the West could indeed be won.

The central plains of North America.

EIGHT

Folklore of the Central Plains

Neighbors and Sharpshooters

Buffalo Bill was a historical figure whose larger-than-life exploits gained him the status of a folk hero.

FEBOLD FEBOLDSON was a Swedish farmer who lived on the Great Plains by himself. He thought he would die of loneliness as the covered wagons rolled by on their way west to Oregon's rich soil and California's gold.

"Stay here! Live here!" he would shout.

"No, this is a terrible place, so flat and dry. We'd just blow away." And on the wagons rolled.

"Wait!" cried Febold. "I promise you some rain soon." It was a tall order, and Febold thought and thought and came up with a hundred ideas. He finally decided on one. He built a huge bonfire beside the lake. It was hot enough that the water in the lake vaporized into clouds over the prairie. The clouds were so big and heavy that when they rolled around and ran into each other, it rained. Buckets and buckets of rain fell. The problem was it never reached the ground, because the air was so hot and dry; the rain turned to steam before it got to the earth. The steam was so thick it was like fog, and the pioneers couldn't see a thing.

"Let's get out of here," the pioneers shouted as they tried to find each other and their wagons.

But Febold bellowed, "Wait, I'll get rid of the fog." He raced to his tool shed and came out with a big pair of hedge clippers.

He cut the fog into strips and plowed it into his field. When the fog was gone, the rain hit the ground. Before you know it, some families agreed to live on the prairie. Febold taught them how to build sod shanties from matted prairie grass and how to fight grasshoppers and survive tornadoes and dust storms.

Now Febold Feboldson could wave and say, "Howdy, neighbors."

NEIGHBORS were very important to the survival of the settlements in the vast, dry prairies. Neighbors cooperated when corn and wheat were planted and harvested, when cattle were branded, and when illness or natural disasters struck. Drought, windstorms, tornadoes, hailstorms that shredded the leaves of corn, and severe winter cold were only some of the hardships endured in the little houses on the prairie.

The Great Plains was the last part of North America to be settled. This area, which stretches from northern Texas and Oklahoma, and includes Nebraska, Kansas, Illinois, the Dakotas, and parts of Colorado, Wyoming, New Mexico, and Montana east of the Rocky Mountains and northward into the prairie provinces of Canada, is one of the largest natural grasslands in the world. This is where the millions of bison and antelope roamed. Cowboys often associated with the Southwest and Texas spent much of their time here, driving large herds of cattle to graze on the plains.

The Plains were the home of some real people who have grown into legends and folk heroes. Annie Oakley, Buffalo Bill Cody, and Wild Bill Hickok are just a few of these real-life people who also became legends.

Most of what is told about the young Wild Bill Hickok is true. He was born James Butler Hickok in Illinois in 1837. When he was 18, he left home and moved to Kansas, where he got a job as a stage driver on the Santa Fe Trail. One night when the stagecoach had a broken axle and the passengers slept under the stars, Wild Bill was nearly killed by a bear. Wild Bill loved fried bacon for breakfast almost every day and he didn't change his clothes

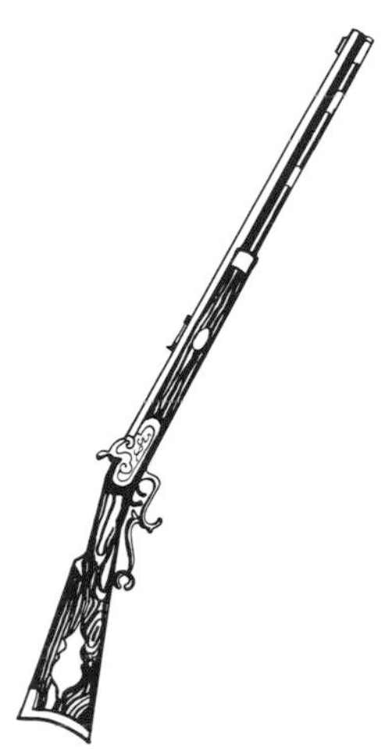

very often, so the bear probably picked out Wild Bill because he smelled like food.

Hickok was a U.S. Marshal for some time, but he was fired for shooting too many people. He was a good liar, and many of the stories of his exploits were exaggerated or totally made up by Wild Bill himself. He tried show business as a traveling ***sharpshooter*** for a while. Eventually, he died in a gunfight in Deadwood, Dakota Territory.

HUMANS with dishonest (and sometimes lethal) intentions, varmints that ate gardens and crops, and poisonous snakes gave the people of the Plains good reason to be skilled with rifles, shotguns, and pistols. Hunting was the best way to put meat on the family's dinner table—but being able to shoot a gun could also save your own or a family member's life.

Annie Oakley came from Ohio and was first recognized as a sharpshooter in her home state. Her amazing ability with guns helped feed her poor family.

Frank Butler, world-renowned champion rifle shooter, traveled to Cincinnati and issued his customary challenge as part of his shooting

Annie Oakley was a legendary sharpshooter.

The eastern seaboard and adjoining states were settled beginning in the 1600s, but the Great Plains were still wild and sparsely populated until the early 1900s. Today the population of the entire state of South Dakota is less than that of the city of Detroit.

The memories of their folk heroes are still fresh in their minds; after all, there are people still alive today who were alive when Buffalo Bill died in 1917 and Annie Oakley in 1926.

exhibition: there would be a hundred-dollar prize to anyone who could outshoot him. Each contestant would shoot 100 rounds and the best score would win.

As the story goes, A. Oakley accepted the challenge and met Frank Butler in Cincinnati. She used her initial so no one would know until she arrived that she was a petite teen-aged girl. Annie shot even with Butler for 99 rounds. On the 100th round, Frank missed. Annie never missed.

Frank and Annie later married and joined Buffalo Bill Cody's Wild West Show. This show was first seen in Omaha, Nebraska, and traveled throughout the Plains and the Southwest. Later, it

FESTIVALS IN THE GREAT PLAINS STATES

National Hobo Music and Poetry Festival—Marquette, Iowa
Woodstock Folk Festival—Woodstock, Illinois
Black Hills Highland Festival and Scottish Games—Sturgis, South Dakota
The Calgary Stampede and Rodeo—Calgary, Alberta, Canada
Crow Fair—the Crow Reservation, Montana

toured the East, playing in New York City, and promoting the great western part of the country as a place to settle and work.

Buffalo Bill Cody got his nickname because he killed more than 4,000 buffalo to feed the workers laying track for the Kansas Pacific Railroad. He was a U.S. Army scout for many years. Despite his history of buffalo slaughter, Buffalo Bill was a man ahead of his time. He believed in conservation and preservation of wild lands. He discouraged killing buffalo for any reason other than the necessity to have food. When asked if women should be able to vote, he replied that they were as well qualified as men. He encouraged women to learn to shoot, using Annie as an example to show that it was not too strenuous or damaging to females. He even voiced an opinion that was radical in the 1800s: women doing equal work should be paid the same as men.

Something about life on the dry, dusty plains may have equalized things for men and women. Working together to make it against nature, they forged a lasting tradition of courage and strength. The legends of these heroes blend fact and fiction, creating larger-than-life figures powerful enough to still inspire our imaginations.

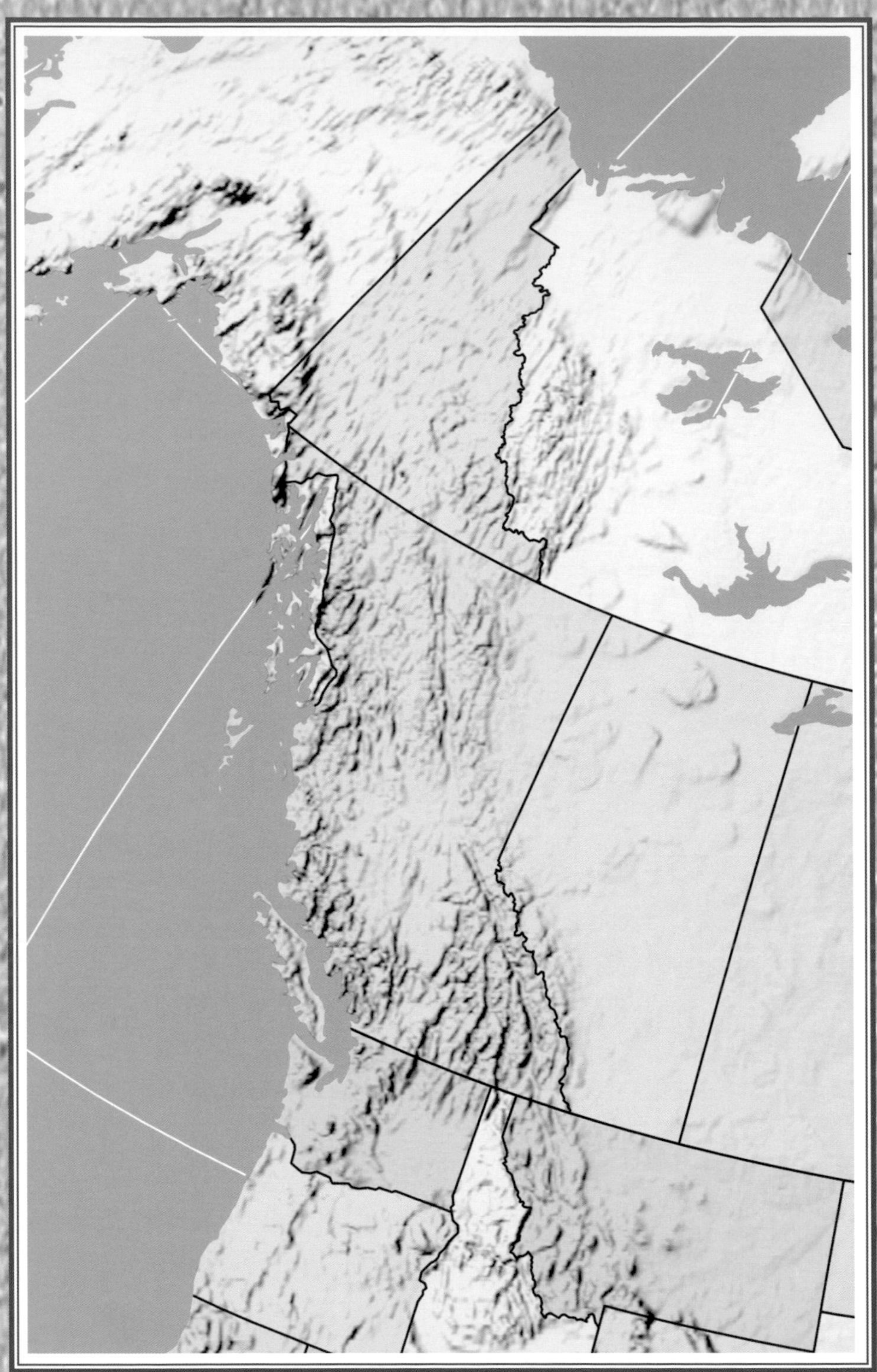

The Northwest.

NINE

Folklore of the Northwest, Including Canada

Nature and Folklore

The "Girl Who Dreamed Geese" is a folktale from the Inuit of the Northwest.

SUPPOSE YOUR life depended on the mysterious marvel of nature known to us as migration. Also suppose you lived at a time when you had no way to explain why animals went away at certain times of the year, or where they went, or why they returned. You only knew that if they did not appear on schedule, your village's way of life was doomed. You might have grown up with a story like this one from Alaska and the Northwest Territories.

A long time ago a young girl lived with her mother and father in a village in the far northwest. She was proud that her ancestors were geese-dreamers. But in the spring of her tenth year, her parents told the village they had quit dreaming geese. Everyone was very upset.

"It has been your family's honor to dream geese for many years. Besides, if you don't dream about them, they will be insulted and might not fly north to our marshes."

"We don't care," said the girl's father. "Geese shedding feathers. Geese honking. We are sick and tired of doing all the geese-dreaming work. No more. Our daughter is old enough to dream geese."

The villagers were frightened and angry. "You have many good years left and your daughter is untrained. We think you are very selfish. We think you should leave the village and go live by yourselves."

The parents were banished, but to everyone's surprise the girl was good at dreaming geese. The flocks came, and the hunters

What is taller than the average man, is covered with hair, has long arms, ape-like hands, and a 15-inch footprint? It also has red, amber, or white eyes. It has been reported to include corn, rabbits, garbage, and apples in its diet but has never actually been seen eating anything.

Give up? Bigfoot or Sasquatch is the answer to this question. This folk creature has been reported living in the Pacific Northwest for many years, and its story is a good example of a folk legend being told, improved upon, and reported in newspapers and on television.

killed what they needed for food. At summer's end, the flocks left for the south.

All was well for three years. But in the spring of the girl's 13th year, her luck changed. Night after night, she dreamed only an empty sky. She tried sleeping in different places in her house and even outside the house, but nothing helped.

A powerful ***shaman*** came to her. "Keep trying," he told her. "Keep trying to dream the geese."

She tried, but still she only dreamed one goose. The villagers paddled out and caught the goose, but the shaman took it away and worked some magic. When he showed it to them again, it was made of twigs. "The girl cannot dream geese. She brought only this one goose and it is wood. She is bad luck and must leave the village. She must go away to the edge of the earth and be a hermit until the end of her days."

The girl wept, but the jealous shaman said he would do the geese-dreaming from then on.

"I will go," sobbed the girl. "If you can dream the geese so the old people will not starve, I will build a hermit hut at the edge of the earth."

The next morning the shaman boasted that he had dreamed geese. But the hunters found none. "No geese! No geese!" they told him.

"I did dream geese!" the shaman cried. "They got confused and forgot how to fly north."

The villagers swatted him with dog harnesses. "Liar!"

"No, no—it's the truth! They were blinded by the moon and are wandering around lost. Tonight I will dream them here."

The hunters didn't believe him. "We must find the girl and give her one more chance. The geese have never been this late, and the shaman has cost precious time with his fake geese-dreaming." They hit the shaman on the head with a cooking pot and tied him up. Then some went to fetch the girl's parents while

Folktales and myths can be found to explain almost every volcano, river, canyon, desert, or island in North America.

The Columbia is a mighty river in the state of Washington, but it wasn't always so. Coyote was walking along one day in the summer sun. "I want a cloud," he demanded. A cloud came and made some shade. "I want more clouds." More clouds came and the sky began to look stormy. Coyote was still hot. "How about some rain?" said Coyote. The clouds sprinkled. Coyote wasn't satisfied. "More rain." The rain became a downpour. "I want a creek to put my feet in." A creek trickled beside him. "It should be deeper," complained Coyote. It became the huge swirling river we know today.

others brought the girl back from the edge of the world.

The mother gave the girl some warm, nourishing broth. "I think I feel well enough to dream the geese down from the moon," the girl whispered. "I hear them and will try to dream them down."

In the morning, the girl reported she had dreamed flocks and flocks of geese. Soon the villagers heard honking, and the geese returned to the marsh. While the villagers had a great feast, the shaman worked loose from the ropes. Not wanting to be kicked and swatted any more, he flew to the moon and stayed there for a long time.

UNLIKE the Inuit people, whose lives depended on the cycles of nature, the hardy settlers who moved west to California, Washington, and Oregon seemed sure of their own ability to sur-

The folklore of the native tribes has shaped the traditions and culture of the Northwest.

FESTIVALS OF THE NORTHWEST

Alaska Folk Festival—Centennial Hall, Juneau, Alaska
Oregon Folklife Festival—Corvallis/Linn-Benton, Oregon
Northwest Folklife Festival—Seattle, Washington
Edmonton Heritage Festival—Edmonton, Alberta
Yukon International Storytelling Festival—Whitehorse, Yukon

vive in the wild country. Rivers and forests, rich land, plentiful game, and a favorable climate put them in good spirits.

As each band of pioneers and adventurers found a new place to settle, they couldn't resist bragging about it to show the folks back home how smart they were to move to the new territory. Northern California is known today as one of the healthiest places to live in the whole country, and apparently the early settlers recognized this, too.

One man was said to have lived to be over 200 years old. He got bored after living so long but just never got sick enough to die. Finally his relatives, who were also getting tired of waiting around for their inheritance, suggested that the old man move out of the state. Sure enough, when he left California he took sick and died.

It was his last request to be buried in California, so his heirs brought his body home. No sooner did they reach his hometown than the old man revived and sat right up in his coffin. His heirs suggested he travel again, but the old gentleman decided to stick it out and let nature take its course.

Humorous tales like this one came from the pioneers who settled in the Northwest, but much of the region's folklore comes from the tribes that lived there before the white newcomers arrived. Settlers adopted the myths, herbal medicine, and weather forecasting traditions of the native people. The tales they created themselves were often humorous, like the one above—or spooky, like the one that follows.

IN 1891, a merchant seaman built a fine house in Oregon. The seaman and his wife and daughter lived there only two years before he had serious financial problems and had to sell their home. The new owner turned it into a hotel for summer visitors.

The attic floor formed the ceiling of the dining room, but the attic itself was cluttered, like many attics today, with old furniture and discarded paintings, and the owners and the hotel staff seldom visited it. Occasionally, though, hotel guests heard footsteps, and sometimes a lady's stockinged feet were seen walking through thin air overhead. They would walk right through the ceiling and up into the attic. Because of the old-fashioned **lisle** stockings, the ghost was thought to be the seaman's dead wife, who was disappointed in having to give up her home.

Over the years the house has changed hands several times, but the feet that walk with no floor beneath them are still heard and seen. Lights go on and off, kitchen appliances break down, candles are snuffed out as people dine in the restaurant, and ingredients are mysteriously

Stories of ghosts are popular everywhere, including the Northwest.

added to soups and sauces. In recent times when lights went on in the restaurant after closing, the police were summoned to investigate. The K-9 dog found nothing on the first or second floor . . . but the dog refused to enter the attic.

Everyone who has ever owned or worked in this building adds to the story. This folk story that started over a hundred years ago is still being told today.

Adults as well as children love a good ghost story. Being scared by a storyteller is a way to experience the thrill of fear in a safe surrounding. While sitting around the campfire or in the meeting hall, at a sewing bee or corn husking, a good spooky tale entertained the early families of this region. Scary stories were easy to create in a day when lanterns cast shadows and the woods were full of strange noises at night. Buildings, before the days of central heat and electricity, creaked and groaned in changing temperatures, and shutters and roof shingles banged and rattled. Perhaps a spooky story was also a good way to discourage children from trespassing in forbidden buildings or from wandering too far from home.

NATURE is often kind in the Northwest. It was revered by the native tribes, and it was considered a bonus by the new settlers who congratulated themselves for choosing to locate in such rich surroundings. And the moist, rich land of the Northwest proved to be fertile ground for folk legends as well.

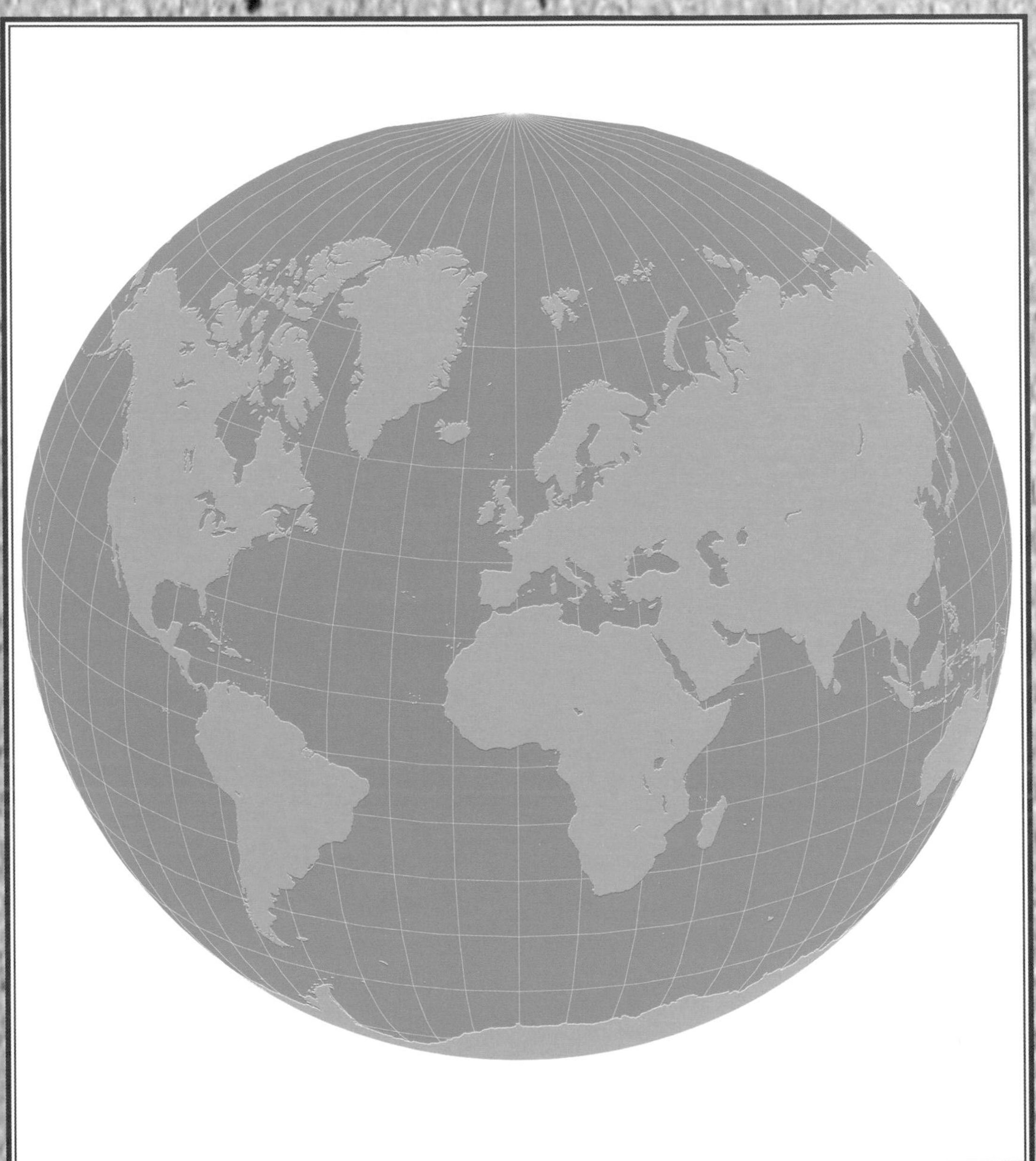

Folklore spans the globe.

TEN

Across Boundaries

Shared Folklore

The story of the "Vanishing Hitchhiker" is told from region to region.

EACH REGION of North America has its own unique flavor, a flavor blended from the weather, the land, and the people who live there. But folklore also has a way of slipping across boundary lines from region to region.

The following tale has been told numerous times and was featured on the television program *Unsolved Mysteries*. No one knows where it started, but it is a myth that resurfaces often in all of North America's regions.

Year 1980: A young man was driving along a dark and lonely road when a pretty teenaged girl stepped out in front of his car. He stopped quickly, barely missing her. She asked for a ride to her home. It was a chilly night, and she shivered in her thin white dress. The young man told her to get in and then loaned her his sweater. Only a few miles down the road, she pointed to the lights of a large house set back at the end of a long winding driveway.

"Let me off here," she said, even though a small section of a cemetery was between them and the house.

The girl ran off without another word, disappearing in the dark of the trees surrounding the graveyard. The young man knew she still had his sweater, but he thought it would be a good excuse to visit her the next day.

In the morning, he drove up to the house. When he asked to see the young lady he had befriended the previous night, the maid told him that only a middle-aged couple resided there. When he described the girl, the maid turned to a portrait in the hall.

"It sounds like Melissa," she said, "But Missy's been dead for six years."

The young man drove out to the road, parked the car, and walked through the cemetery. On Melissa's tombstone he found his sweater.

Folklore is not learned from a book the way you might study dates in history or math facts. Instead, folklore is learned as you grow in your family and community. Folklore is learned by living it.

YEAR 1950: In Shiprock, New Mexico, a Navajo man went to a village dance. After some traditional Indian dances were performed, a local disc jockey played modern dance music. The young people were having a good time when a sudden thunderstorm arose. A cold rain fell, and the Navajo man saw that his partner was wet and shivering. She said she had not been to a dance in a long time and was from another nearby village. He put his windbreaker over her and offered to drive her to her ***hogan***. He dropped her off, and she disappeared into a hogan, still wearing his jacket over her head in the pouring rain.

The next day the man drove to the girl's home. An old woman came out of the next hogan and asked what he wanted.

"I came to get my jacket that I lent to the girl who lives over there," he replied.

"No one lives there now. It is all locked up. See for yourself.

There was a young girl who lived there, but she died and is buried in the floor of the house," the old woman told him.

The man peered through a crack in the wooden plank door and saw a mound in the earthen floor. He also saw his jacket hanging on a peg on the wall.

Now let's go back even farther—and let's leave North America and cross the globe to the year 1798, Russia: A young soldier was driving his troika (three horses pulling a sleigh) in a snowstorm when he spotted a young lady struggling through the drifts. He offered to take her home and wrapped a fur shawl around her shoulders.

"Let me out here." She pointed to a grove of trees that shielded the nearby cottage. "My father is very strict." Despite the soldier's protests, she climbed down into the snow and disappeared in the swirling flakes.

The next day the soldier made a proper call at the cottage to see the girl again. When he asked about her, the woman who answered the door began to weep.

"My daughter left the house years ago after a disagreement with her father. She was killed by wolves that same night as she hid in the forest over there."

The soldier walked to the trees. His fur robe lay carefully folded near a wooden grave marker.

A similar tale is told in China and most likely in other regions around the world. The similarity between the stories is a mystery. Did a tale cross the oceans hundreds of years ago and become adapted to the surroundings of local people as it traveled? Did all the regions have

Folklore travels the roads of North America.

a need to tell this kind of story? Do all humans' minds work alike when it comes to imaginative folktales?

This story isn't the only one to span the regions of the world. In earlier chapters we mentioned Bigfoot who lives in the North American Northwest and the Devil that lives in New Jersey. But did you know that Florida has its Skunk Ape as well? In Asia the Abominable Snowman, or Yeti, is the equivalent of a Sasquatch. Australia is home to another cousin called the Yowie. Europe calls this man-ape a Kaptar, and Africans call it Kikomba. Sightings of mysterious man-shaped creatures have been reported in distant regions of the globe ever since the time of Marco Polo's journeys. So again the question arises: are these creatures real or has the human imagination always loved to play with the truth in the same ways?

We may never know the answer. While we ponder this mystery (right this moment, even as you read), children are learning games and rhymes from other children; teenagers are playing the same jokes on underclassmen that their parents played; and older people are repeating the same old stories they learned from their grandparents. All across the regions of North America, folklore is alive and well.

Further Reading

The National Association for the Preservation and Perpetuation of Storytelling. *Best Loved Stories Told at the National Storytelling Festival, 20th Anniversary Edition*. Jonesborough, Tenn.: National Storytelling Press, 1991.

———. *More Best Loved Stories Told at the National Storytelling Festival, 20th Anniversary Edition*. Jonesborough, Tenn.: National Storytelling Press, 1992.

Norman, Howard. *The Girl Who Dreamed Only Geese*. New York: Harcourt Brace, 1997.

Peck, Catherine, editor. *QPB Treasury of North American Folktales*. New York: Quality Paperback Book Club, 1998.

Sanna, Ellyn. *Ethnic Folklore*. Philadelphia: Mason Crest, 2003.

Sorenson, Ruth. *Beyond the Prairie Wind: History, Folklore and Traditions from Denmark, Kansas*. Hillsboro, Kan.: Partnership Book Services, 1996.

For More Information

www.americanfolklore.net
A tall tale for each state and many folk personalities easily found by category.

www.crt.state.la.us/folklife
One of many state university sites with references to folklore.

www.folkworld.de/frog/canfst.htm
FROG—Folk and Roots Online Guide

www.google.com
Search Les Voyageurs sites in French and English. Some French sites will be translated into English and are very entertaining.

www.prairieghosts.com
The complete story of the Lost Dutchman Mine is found here.

www.readthewest.com
Calamity Jane and others are given a humorous touch while untangling fact from fiction.

www.sandiego-books.com
Hundreds of folk cures and superstitions listed.

Glossary

Bayou A swampy river.
Emissaries Representative or agent.
Flotillas A fleet of ships or boats.
Frontier The edge of civilization.
Hatch The covering over a hole in a ship's deck.
Hogan A Navajo dwelling made from mud and logs.
Hysteria Overwhelming fear and strong emotion.
Jib-boom A spar on the bow of a ship.
Kiln An oven or furnace used for drying or firing a substance.
Lisle A cotton fabric.
Nostalgia A feeling of longing for the past.
Parish A division of local government in Louisiana.
Prospectors People who search for gold or other ores.
Shaman A medicine man.
Sharecroppers Tenant farmers who receive a share of the crops as well as credit for seed, tools, and living quarters, in return for their labor.
Sharpshooter A good marksperson.

Index

Biographies

Ann Vitale lives in rural northeastern Pennsylvania with a Newfoundland dog and a calico cat. She also intentionally feeds many birds, chipmunks, and squirrels—but the deer, bears, possums and other critters just drop in whenever they are in the neighborhood. She has been a 4-H leader for 25 years in the dog-training project.

Dr. Alan Jabbour is a folklorist who served as the founding director of the American Folklife Center at the Library of Congress from 1976 to 1999. Previously, he began the grant-giving program in folk arts at the National Endowment for the Arts (1974–1976). A native of Jacksonville, Florida, he was trained at the University of Miami (B.A.) and Duke University (M.A., Ph.D.). A violinist from childhood on, he documented old-time fiddling in the Upper South in the 1960s and 1970s. A specialist in instrumental folk music, he is known as a fiddler himself, an art he acquired directly from elderly fiddlers in North Carolina, Virginia, and West Virginia. He has taught folklore and folk music at UCLA and the University of Maryland and has published widely in the field.